# Tarot

## A Beginner's Guide to Understanding the Tarot

*Lauren Lingard*

# Table of Contents

Introduction ............................................................................. 1

Chapter One: Getting Started ................................................ 6

Chapter Two: The Major Arcana ......................................... 10

Chapter Three: The Royal Court Cards ............................... 55

Chapter Four: The Other Court Cards ................................. 90

Chapter Five: Three Easy Spreads for Beginners ............. 173

Chapter Six: Reading the Cards ......................................... 186

Conclusion .......................................................................... 193

# Introduction

*"With a deck of cards, we can tell the stories of where we come from, how it is that we are here, what awaits us and what we will or might become."*

-Wald Amberstone, tarotschool.com

Imagine a friend who is always there to hold your hand, help you through the difficult times and celebrate with you when things go well. Imagine that this friend is your biggest supporter and, sometimes, the only friend who has the courage to tell you what you need to hear, rather than what you want to hear.

If this sounds like the sort of friend you would like to welcome into your life and keep with you forever, then you are now in the right place. From the very moment your first-ever Tarot deck sits in your hands, waiting to be unwrapped and cherished, you have found that friend.

Soon, you will find you have stepped into a world that, while sometimes still misunderstood, could hold the key to helping you make all the important decisions that will shape your life.

This does not mean that the Tarot cards themselves decide what will happen to you.

The cards, as you will learn as you work your way through this book, will simply act as your guides in this adventure we call life. Once you know what the cards are saying, it is for you to decide whether or not you want to pay heed, carry on along the same path, or choose a whole new direction.

You can think of the cards as your allies, friends who are always on your side but who are only able to speak to you through symbols and imagery. Your job then is to learn how to understand what the cards are saying through those images.

Let's take one example and a card that those who are not familiar with the Tarot will dread seeing turn up in a reading. That card is Death, whose very presence in the deck is often the reason people fear the Tarot and may be anxious about even having a deck in the house.

It is human nature to feel scared of what we don't know, but it is common sense to diffuse that fear by educating ourselves.

If you already have your own Rider Waite Tarot deck, shuffle through and find this card. If not, don't worry. You can see for yourself that the image of a skeleton riding on a white horse across broken bodies strewn over a battlefield is an image that, without any deeper understanding, looks alarming.

However, in the Tarot, the card that depicts Death does not mean death at all.

As one professional Tarot reader I know well likes to say, "If you are dying, you probably already know it and don't need a card to tell you that's what is going on with you."

She has a macabre sense of humour. And she can afford to be humorous because she also knows Death can be one of the most liberating cards in the entire deck because while it is true it can mean the end (death) of something, it *always* signifies the start (birth) of something else.

You can understand this by thinking about a time when you had to let one thing go to get another thing that you wanted more. Maybe this was a new job or a new home or a new relationship. You will have stepped into the new with perhaps a tinge of sadness for the departure of the old.

Now look again at the Death card. Can you see the sun rising in the background on the far right-hand side of the card? And just in front of that sun, can you see the figure of a bishop blessing what has died and gone before? He is welcoming Death as the first step in the creation of something new.

This then is the true and deeper interpretation of just one of the cards in the Tarot deck.

There are 77 more cards for you to discover and learn about as you deepen your understanding of how Tarot can work powerfully for you, to guide you now and forever through all of your life choices.

You will learn, with this book, how to interpret the cards and how they reflect what has happened, what is happening now, and what could happen to you in your life.

As you practice the spreads we use to read the cards in the correct order, remember you are looking for clues about archetypal themes, other people, and important transitions, all of which make up life's rich tapestry.

See yourself as a detective being trained to look for and interpret those clues, and then have fun making your own relationship to the cards which will, inevitably, result in you developing meanings that are unique to your understanding of the Tarot.

Welcome, then, to the wonderful world of the Tarot and to this introduction to all the magical cards in the Tarot deck. They are just waiting to meet you through the pages of this book for beginners.

# Chapter One: Getting Started

**The Origins of the Tarot**

The Tarot was invented in Italy in the 1430s when someone–nobody knows precisely who–added a fifth suit of 21 new cards to the existing four. They called this new suit the *trionfi,* meaning "triumphs."

These were the cards that are now known as the Major Arcana and in chapter two, you can learn about each of these cards, what they mean, why they are so important in Tarot readings and how, whatever other cards show up in a reading, they "trump," or triumph, over what has gone before and what lies ahead.

After their invention, the Tarot deck was used primarily to play regular card games and so it would be another almost 400 years before a Frenchman by the name of Jean-Baptiste Alliette published the first formal guide to using the Tarot for divination or "cartomancy," which just means fortune-telling using cards.

Using the pseudonym *Etteilla,* Jean-Baptiste says he drew heavily from the *Book of Thoth* - an ancient Egyptian book of wisdom said to have been written by the god Thoth–to ascribe symbols and meanings to each of the cards in the Tarot deck. He incorporated beliefs about each of the four elements and astrology and released his own revised deck. He was also the first to prescribe a specific order to the cards and to the way they could be laid out in a spread for the purpose of divination. And so, in that sense, Jean-Baptiste Alliette is now acknowledged as the world's first-ever professional Tarot reader.

Fast-forward two more centuries and Tarot underwent another major reinvention with the publication of the Rider Waite deck in 1910. This was the late Victorian era and in Britain, where this new deck was first conceived of, there was a lot of interest in all things esoteric and occult. And so, it was against this backdrop that the American-born British poet and scholarly mystic, Arthur Edward Waite, who was at that time a member of an esoteric group called the

Order of the Golden Dawn, had the idea to completely reinvent the Tarot deck.

He worked with another member of the Golden Dawn group, the American theater designer and artist Pamela Colman-Smith who devised the artwork for the new deck. Arthur Waite then took her new illustrations for the cards, along with his book, *A Key To The Tarot*, to the publisher William Rider who put his and Waite's name to the deck but left Pamela's off.

Poor Pamela died alone, penniless, and unrecognized for her artistic talents in Pimlico, London, in 1951, so it is an extraordinary tribute to her talents that the Rider Waite deck is still the one most commonly used in Tarot readings today.

**How We Use Tarot Today**

When people think of Tarot cards and Tarot readings, they often imagine a mysterious world of fortune-telling, with the cards revealing what lies ahead regardless of their own life choices and preferences. For those who think of it that way, the Tarot may seem a little scary.

The truth is, the Tarot will only tell you what your subconscious already knows. The real value in learning more about the cards and their symbology is to make that bridge with your subconscious and understand what your Higher Self or your Soul is trying to communicate.

The Tarot will not tell you definitively what is going to happen to you, rather it can be used as guidance to explore what will likely happen if you stay on a particular path, divert to another, or even just take time to think about what has already happened to you and why.

In other words, you can use the Tarot cards to initiate a dialogue with your hidden self and to try and learn more about all aspects of your life. This can include your love life, your work, your finances, your friendships, and your longer-term goals and dreams.

Nothing in life is set in stone, and the Tarot can only tell you what is likely to happen. Once you become aware of possible outcomes, you may then decide on a different path and in that way, those outcomes will change.

Working with the Tarot is like working with a therapist. Sometimes it will feel as if there is nowhere to hide, but don't shy away from what the Tarot is revealing to you. Facing what is really going on is the only way of guaranteeing you are making informed choices and you are the one in the driver's seat of your life.

**Choosing Your Tarot Deck**

There are Tarot decks based on Native American symbology, Faery magic, the Druid pathway, Astrology, the works of Jung, and even a deck called The Zombie Tarot, so it can seem confusing knowing which deck is right for you. My advice is to forget about this and just allow the right deck to find you at the right time.

There is a saying which is often used in esoteric circles which says, "When the student is ready, the teacher will come." And the same can be said about the Tarot. The right deck will find you when you are ready but until then, if you are a beginner, stick with the Rider Waite.

This book is based solely on the Classical Rider Waite Tarot deck and will show you how to interpret each of the 78 cards in the deck by looking closely at each illustration and understanding the symbols depicted. You will find this is in itself an excellent training for transferring the same interpretative skills to any new deck that you may feel resonates more with you, as you advance in your understanding of the Tarot.

## Stepping Out on This Adventure

You may notice, when your own deck arrives, that the modern Tarot contains 22 Major Arcana cards, not 21, because at some point The Fool was added to the new suit.

The Fool represents the start of a journey, and so if you were to choose a card for your decision to learn more about Tarot by reading this book and perhaps buying your own Tarot deck, then it would be The Fool.

Of course, this card does not mean foolish at all but indicates someone starting out on a venture with very little knowledge of what lies ahead. This is precisely what you are doing now, so you can already see how the cards are a clever metaphor for life itself.

## Chapter Summary

We have learned a little of the origins and history of the Tarot. We discovered the most important part of learning to read the cards is to understand they speak to us in symbols and imagery. We need to learn to see deeply into these images so we can interpret their meaning as it applies to the question we are asking the cards.

In the next chapters, you will meet the cards and begin to decipher their meanings.

# Chapter Two: The Major Arcana

**The Mysterious Fifth Suit**

The Major Arcana are the cards that make up that fifth suit which made its first appearance in the Italian decks of playing cards in the 1430s. As we learned from the history of Tarot in the previous chapter, these are the *trionfi* or "triumphs," which indicate something of great significance happening or about to happen.

If you are a card player and have ever played a game like Top Trumps, you already know that a trump card is superior in power to all the other cards you may have in your hand. When it comes to the Tarot the same interpretation applies.

As we learned in the introduction to the book, all Tarot cards reveal something to us about the central themes, transits, and people in our lives. We may also think about how we embody a particular archetype that shows up in a Tarot reading to benefit from the power that archetype can bring.

Pay close attention to the Major Arcana when they turn up and think about how the qualities they represent can help you to fully realize your desires and achieve your life goals.

**Understanding The Major Arcana**

THE FOOL

### The Fool: Number Zero

There's a child-like quality about The Fool who is setting off on his life journey with all his worldly goods in a knotted handkerchief. He carries a white rose, which means a love of life, and he clearly hasn't a care in the world, but that's because he's not looking where he is going! Look at his feet. One more step and he'll be over the cliff edge.

Luckily, he has his little white dog with him. The dog represents his instinct and will stop him from plunging to his death. When this card shows up, it tells us we are the start of something, which always means being at the end of something else. The Fool shows up when we start the journey to become who we are meant to be and reminds us to trust our intuition.

THE MAGICIAN

## The Magician: Number One

With his feet planted on the ground, the Magician reaches for the heavens to draw down the divine energy. Look closely at his table; he has all four symbols of the Tarot suits on it. Some say this is the most powerful card in the deck, because this man is not messing around. This card is about initiation, power, alchemy, and magic. Change is coming and it will be a big change. What was negative can become positive. What was sad can be transformed into happiness. This is a card of action.

## The High Priestess: Number Two

The spiritual teacher and seeker, the High Priestess shows a devout woman crowned by a moonstone sitting between the pillars of good and evil and guarding the gateway to the fruits of knowledge and wisdom that lie just behind her. She is the female match to the Magician, but where he knows how to do things, her knowledge is all about what, why, and when. She represents hidden depths and hidden knowledge. Psychic and intuitive, she is a teacher, but also still a student of life. When she shows up in a reading, she is saying it is time to retreat and think further about a situation.

THE EMPRESS

## The Empress: Number Three

This is the card of creation. It can indicate someone is planning to start a family or a new business, embark on a new relationship, or take classes to learn a new skill. For women, this card represents you and for heterosexual men, it refers to your mother or mate. This is a mature woman surrounded by an abundance of nature. She is pregnant with possibility. When she shows up, your job is to discover what it is you are meant to be creating or nurturing. She is the card of all things maternal and signifies success if you are on the verge of creating something new.

THE EMPEROR

## The Emperor: Number Four

Just as the Empress speaks to us of maternal influence and archetypes, the Emperor represents the paternal: father, responsibility, and the law. The long white beard of the mature man we see depicted suggests hard-won wisdom, and if you look closely, you will see he sits on a throne adorned by two ram heads. The ram is the sign of fiery Mars, so this is a man who means business. In a reading, he can signify all kinds of powers, from an authoritarian establishment to the power of your own determination. He may signal leadership and promotion. In a man's reading, he may reflect his father or a male partner. In a woman's reading he may be her father or, if she is heterosexual, her partner. The Emperor in a reading says you are now in charge of your life and can enjoy a level of security you have earned through your own hard work and dedication.

**The Hierophant: Number Five**

Sometimes called the Pope card, the Hierophant sits on a throne with the keys of heaven between his feet and with two acolytes at his feet awaiting his blessing or teachings. This is the card of convention and tradition, so if the subject of the reading has a relationship, it will likely be a traditional one, perhaps a marriage. The Hierophant also shows up when we are in need of a teacher or wise words from someone who can take up a counselling role in our lives. He can indicate changes are afoot, but these will be changes grounded in higher learning, including deepening our spiritual or religious beliefs.

## The Lovers: Number Six

There is always a frisson of excitement when this enamored pair shows up in a reading. It is tempting to think romantic love with a capital L is about to bowl you over and sweep you along in its fairytale. This may happen, but the deeper meaning of this card is usually that a choice that relates to love may have to be made, and when it is, something may be lost forever. If, for example, you are single and agree to date someone who is interested in you, then love may grow between you and what you will both give up is your single selves. The Lovers can also indicate there may be a difficult choice to be made over matters of the heart or even that temptation has appeared within a loving relationship. The couple we see look like Adam and Eve in the Garden of Eden, and it may be that the choices you make now will close doors behind you for good, so don't make them lightly.

## The Chariot: Number Seven

Seven is the number of both magic and karma, so when the Chariot is one of your cards you can expect the unexpected. With this card we see a princely figure driving a chariot pulled by two muscular sphinxes, one black, one white. The white sphinx speaks to us of the good experiences we have and the black of those that are more challenging. The trick is not to become derailed by either, but to accept your karma and drive a steady straight path through the middle. You will succeed, as long as you stay on the path of acceptance.

## Strength: Number Eight

Look how gently the woman depicted in this card is closing the mouth of the powerful lion. She shows us that strength lies not in force but in gentleness and kindness. What this card really tells us is that here is a person who has the courage to face the lion as themselves. They have no weapons or armor for protection, but bring a kind and brave heart to the circumstances that are being considered in the reading. She remains calm and gentle and somehow dominant over the lion. This card tells us that strength of character can quietly and positively influence the outcome of a situation. If this card appears in a reading that is concerned with recovery from illness or injury, it bodes well for a full recovery.

## The Hermit: Number Nine

We see a lonely and stooped cloaked figure standing on cold snow-covered ground, raising his lantern to light the way ahead. What is he looking for? We need to know because if this card is in your reading, then it tells us what you are looking for and how you will find it. He is looking for wisdom and he is telling you that this is a journey you must take alone. You won't find what you are seeking in a crowd or the distraction of company. You need to withdraw and look within. Solitude, meditation, and soul-searching will all help you find the answers you seek, but to do this, you need to withdraw from society for a while. That's the only way to find the path that is already lit for you. The Hermit frequently shows up in the reading of someone who has become a great teacher and who can inspire others just by living their authentic life choices.

WHEEL of FORTUNE

## The Wheel of Fortune: Number Ten

If this card makes you feel like life is like a game show, then you're not wrong! Spin the wheel of life now, because you are guaranteed when this card shows up that life is about to change for you for the better! The wheel we are looking at represents life, and the four images in each corner of the card represent the four elements of earth, air, fire, and water. If you have been unlucky in love, that's about to change. If you have been struggling with money, expect a financial windfall. You are poised for a change in status or position, and when this card shows up, the only way is up!

## Justice: Number Eleven

The woman in the picture has a sword in one hand and balancing scales in the other. It's not always clear what she is about to do. She is definitely concerned with fairness and balance, but it seems she won't think twice about metaphorically chopping your head off if there is a transgression from these core values. That makes sense because Justice is all about truth, empowerment, and balance. She is inviting you to step forward as your true, authentic self, and to drop the B.S. You might need to wield your metaphorical sword and cut ties with anyone who is taking you further away from your true purpose. You will know if this is the case; she is just telling you to recognize it and act. If your question is about something you have no control over, this card tells you the outcome will be just, even if it is not one you hoped for.

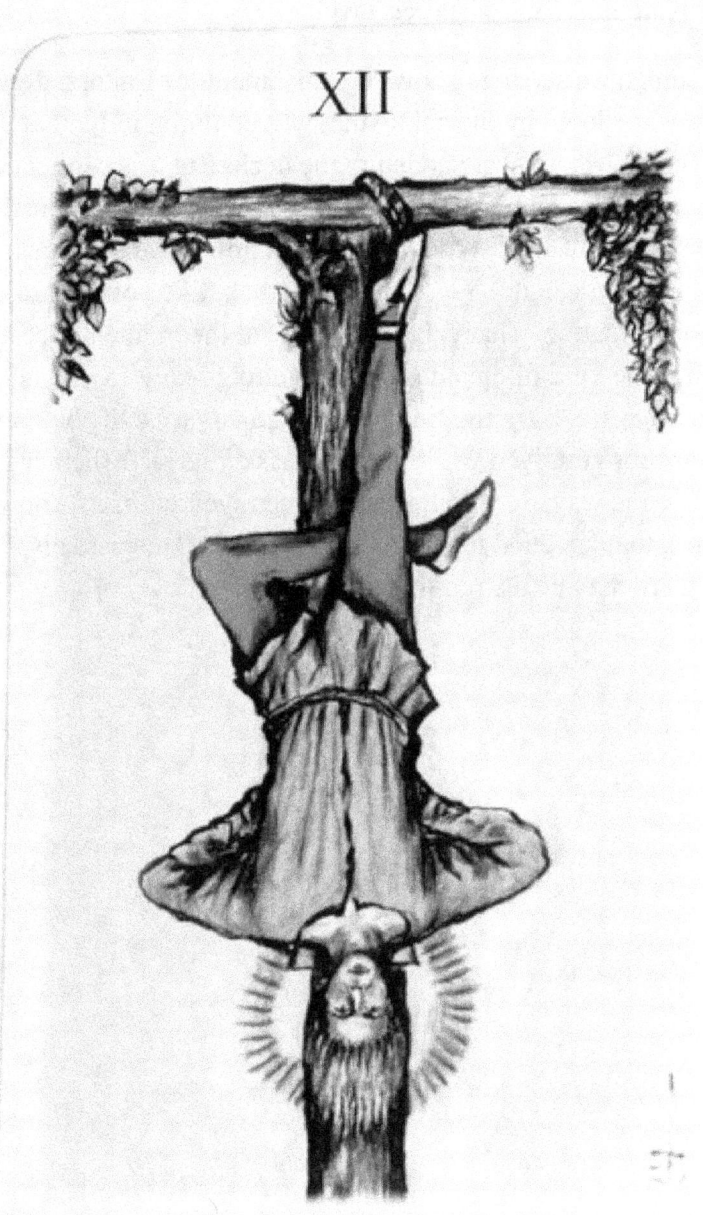

## The Hanged Man: Number Twelve

The image we see here shows a punishment for traitors, death by hanging upside down by the ankle, that was common in Italy at the time the Major Arcana were added to the deck. But this card does not mean you are going to be punished. It may reveal you *feel* punished over something, but its real message is "Let go," because there is nothing more you can do. You likely feel stuck, like you cannot change your situation. That is probably true at the moment, because you are in some kind of metamorphosis, getting ready for the next change in your life. Stop fighting it. Let it go and trust the outcome will be right for you. And while you wait, ask yourself whether there have been some ways in which you have betrayed yourself, and your core values, that have led to you feeling so stuck. This card also suggests there may be a struggle with depression.

## Death: Number Thirteen

This is another card that sends a ripple of fear around the room, but it does not mean death looms, other than in the way we know death will eventually come to us all. If death is more imminent you will already know that, and you don't need the Tarot to tell you! We see an armored skeleton riding amongst the dead: kings, queens, commoners, and even children. In the Tarot, Death is the card that tells us something is about to end. It could be a job or a relationship or the end of where you have been living. This is a card of change and transformation because what follows death is a rebirth and a new beginning. If you have been unsure about letting something go, this card encourages you to find the courage to do so. It is the single most important card that indicates transformation, so let it do its work. Remember, when we look at the image, there is a Bishop shown in the foreground giving his blessing to this impending ending.

## Temperance: Number Fourteen

With this card we see an angelic figure standing barefoot in a lagoon and pouring water from one chalice to another. The figure is androgynous, neither male not female, and is focused only on making sure both vessels contain the same amount of liquid so that there is a fair balance. This then tells us Temperance is always about balance. It is telling the reader to avoid extremes and to walk the middle path. Forget either/or scenarios and find a way to live with both. This card tells us to find a way to integrate things so we can choose moderation and keep our emotions and our spiritual and physical lives balanced and strong. This card often shows up when we are feeling wobbly about something and reminds us that we can regulate our emotions and allow them to pass through us.

## The Devil: Number Fifteen

The devilish figure who dominates this card has no intention of breaking those chains that we see keeping the enslaved man and woman at his feet, but remember, the Tarot shows us archetypes. In this case, it is one of an unhealthy codependency or addiction. This is a card that depicts negativity, but do not lose hope because look again at those chains and you will see just how easy it will be to escape them and slip away once you decide to do so. This may mean leaving a person or a job that is not right for you or keeping an unhealthy family relationship at arm's length in order to free yourself. The message of this card is to stop enslaving yourself in the chains of self-imposed restrictions. Break free and find the light again.

## The Tower: Number Sixteen

One of the most difficult cards in the entire deck, this one pulls no punches as it warns your life as you know it, or some important aspect of it, is about to collapse. We see the fiery flames burning down from the top of what was once a solid tower and the terrified inhabitants throwing themselves to the ground to escape being burned alive. Will they die anyway on impact with the ground? We don't know. But we do know they have no choice. They cannot survive the inferno which will bring that tower crashing down, leaving rubble and smoldering ash in its wake. So, what this card tells you is that change will be forced upon you. It may show up in an unhappy relationship where both parties are too scared to look outside their misery and break free. This card says well, don't worry because if you won't make the break, we will do it for you by making it impossible for you to stay. This is the card of forewarning, and forewarned is forearmed!

## The Star: Number Seventeen

You may now be starting to have more of an understanding that a Tarot reading tells a story: if the reading is yours, the story is yours too. The Star is the card of great healing and so follows on from both the Devil (enslavement) and the Tower (collapse and change) because healing is what you will need in order to recover from a major life blow. This is a beautiful card that promises healing by helping you to let go of all the emotions that have been holding you back. Have you allowed your life to become derailed from your true purpose because other people have told you that you are not enough? They are lying. The Star archetype promises you it's possible to heal, make a deeper connection with your spiritual purpose, and move your life to a more secure, healthier, and happier higher ground.

## The Moon: Number Eighteen

Since our bodies are made up of more water than anything else, it is inevitable that something that controls the tides–the moon–can affect the tides of our emotions too. We see a domestic dog and a wild wolf both howling at the moon, but there is something else, something that feels more sinister, crawling up the bank from the bottom of the river that flows on to the ocean. It looks like a crayfish or some other form of lower consciousness, and it is there to remind us we don't always know or see what may be present. The Moon is the card that speaks to us of illusion and obfuscation. Is there something in your life that doesn't make sense, but you can't work out why? Are you misunderstanding some part of this truth or are you ignoring the truth by lying to yourself? What is really going on?

## The Sun: Number Nineteen

When the Sun follows the Moon, morning dawns, and we have a new day of possibilities given to us once more. It is as if we have stepped out of the shadowy obfuscation of moonlight into the bright and cheerful glare of the full sun. With this card we see a happy child riding bareback on a pony under the watchful gaze of the sun. There is an abundance of towering and healthy sunflowers in the background. This is a card of success and vibrancy, of vitality and freedom. Whatever it is you are working toward as a goal, it will be yours.

## Judgement: Number Twenty

This card shows us, literally, a clarion call, so sudden and loud it has woken the dead from their coffins. The keyword for this card is "awakening." Your awakening. Do you need some kind of wakeup call? Have you been drifting along making do, simply hoping there may be something better for you around the corner? This card is shouting at you. It is saying stop wasting time, stop wasting your life, and start working toward those goals that are your true desires and dreams. If that means ditching a long-dead marriage or quitting a mind-numbing job, do it. Your happiness is your responsibility and rebirth awaits you.

# XXI

THE WORLD

### The World: Number Twenty-One

Welcome to your new vision of your life! You are, at this moment, in the right time and the right place to make that vision a reality. Everything is stacked in your favor. Now is the time to grab any new opportunity, either in work or in your personal life, and to take another huge step toward becoming who you are meant to be. The woman we see depicted in this card is dancing with joy, and so should you be, because there will be a slight pause and then off you go into the next new and exciting chapter of your life, setting off once again, just like the Fool and his little white dog, to find the path that has been waiting for you all along.

## Chapter Summary

In this chapter, we took a closer look at all 22 cards that make up the fifth suit, or the Major Arcana. We should now understand the archetypes and transitions each of them represents. We can also see that there is a metaphysical journey the Tarot tells us, from stepping out to find adventure as the Fool to celebrating our success and pausing before we do it all again when we draw the World card.

In the next chapters we will explore the significance of the Minor Arcana, starting with the Court Cards.

# Chapter Three: The Royal Court Cards

If the Major Arcana suit speaks to us of big stereotypes and transitions and of the important people influencing or sharing our lives, the Minor Arcana cards do the same, but they also drill down into much more of the detail of our everyday lives–what has gone before and what lies ahead.

There are 56 of these Minor Arcana cards which include 16 court cards with a Page, Knight, Queen, and King for each suit.

Although the court cards are matched in terms of status–the Queen of Swords, for example, is not more or less influential than the Queen of Cups–these two cards carry very different meanings. We will work our way suit-by-suit to familiarize ourselves with the court cards of the Rider Waite Tarot deck.

Each suit is assigned its own element, which links it to astrology, because each astrological sign is also governed by one of the four elements.

We are still only in Chapter Three, but you should be starting to see how we combine multiple clues that are revealed in a Tarot reading to tell us more about the person asking the question, the influences playing out in their life, and the themes and transitions that weave together to make the narrative of their journey.

## Wands (also known as Staffs or Staves)

The Wands represent Fire, and Fire signifies passion, communication, and creativity. Fire is deemed to be masculine and active. The astrological fire signs are: Aries, Sagittarius, and Leo.

If a reading is dominated by wands, you may be reading for someone who is one of these three astrological signs. It may also be someone who works in the creative industries and someone who feels things passionately.

These are all clues you can look for and work with to deliver a more in-depth reading of the cards.

**Reading Wands: The Royal Court Cards**

KING of WANDS

### King

We see an authoritative figure sitting on a throne decorated with two signs of strength, the lion, and the salamander. The latter is eating its own tale which is a sign of infinity. The King holds a blossoming staff (wand), which represents passion and creativity. His robe is fiery red, and his crown is fashioned into tongues of fire. In fact, this is someone who may speak with a forked tongue!

QUEEN of WANDS

**Queen**

Look at the detail in this card to decipher its meaning. Our Queen sits strong and upright on her throne. She holds a sunflower, which is a symbol of success and fertility. Her blossoming wand symbolizes life. At her feet we see a black cat, which tells us she has hidden depths and even witchy ways of seeing what lies ahead. She is warm, welcoming, and trustworthy.

KNIGDS of WANDS

**Knight**

All fiery plumage and held-back energy, our armored Knight and his powerful horse are fired up and raring to gallop on to their next destination. They are both prepared to face what lies ahead and have harnessed energy and enthusiasm to get started. This card often indicates someone is about to move house. It also suggests there are new projects and travel on the horizon.

PAGE of WANDS

**Page**

This is a young man (or woman) at the start of the adventure of life. The arid desert behind indicates their ideas have not yet been brought to fruition, and perhaps they are slightly hesitant and lacking in confidence to take the next step. It is as if they are waiting for a sign, for some kind of reassuring communication that they can take that next step, and all will be well.

## Cups (sometimes called Chalices)

The cups in the Tarot represent water, and water represents emotions. So, any card that forms a part of this suit speaks to us of our feelings; both those we share and those we hide.

Water is said to be feminine and receptive, but remember, over 70% of our bodies, regardless of gender, are made up of water. The astrological signs that link to this element are Cancer, Scorpio, and Pisces.

If the reading is dominated by cups, you are reading for someone who feels all their feelings powerfully and who may allow their heart to rule their head.

**Reading Cups: The Royal Court Cards**

KING of CUPS

**King**

A deeply emotional and caring man, the King of Cups can be guilty of indecision, especially to avoid hurting anyone's feelings. This is a sensitive person with a calm exterior that may be hiding an inner turmoil you would not have guessed at. Is he too emotional? Sometimes. He can also sulk if he does not get his way and is not beyond manipulating others to achieve his goals.

QUEEN of CUPS

**Queen**

She is a dark horse, keeping her deepest feelings locked in the ancient vessel she is holding in her lap, which is known as a yarg. Like our Queen, the yarg has many hidden components, and you cannot access one without working out how to access the other. Like the King, she's sensitive and affectionate, but she won't reveal her true feelings for a long time, if ever.

KNIGDS of CUPS

**Knight**

Where the Knight of Wands is all about fire, passion, and unbridled energy, the Knight of Cups is the embodiment of emotional restraint. He is looking out across the river ahead which he knows he must cross but he is giving nothing away. This card often appears when someone has been so badly hurt that they've learned to keep all their emotions in check and their heart under lock and key.

PAGE of CUPS

**Page**

We see a sensitive young man looking at the fish that has popped its head up out of the chalice he is holding. This is a card that shows up when you may be worried about a younger person, but actually your worry is misplaced, and you are underestimating their resilience. Try to take a more realistic look at why you are concerned for them. Your worries are likely misplaced.

# Swords (also known as Knives or Blades)

The Swords represent thought and intellect. They show up in readings when there is a decision to be made, perhaps one that calls for a ruthless and non-emotional assessment of what needs to be done.

These are the cards of the air and link to the astrological air signs of Libra, Aquarius, and Gemini. Air, like fire, is deemed masculine and active, so these cards speak to the need for decisive action.

The Swords also represent pain, and when a reading is dominated by Swords, it is a sign there have been many sorrows in the life of the person asking the question of the cards.

**Reading Swords: The Royal Court Cards**

KING of SWORDS

**King**

The King of Swords knows we can only find our way to the truth by sticking to the facts, and he urges you to stay neutral and do your homework before making a decision. He radiates intellectual power and authority, and tells you that clear-headed thinking is the way forward for you. He may seem cold and even ruthless, but he has the courage to do what needs to be done.

QUEEN of SWORDS

## Queen

Here is the archetype for an older and wiser form of female energy, one that does not suffer fools. She has compassion–she is holding her left hand out toward you–but, like the King, she has learned that the truth will serve you better than a rollercoaster of unwieldy emotions. She is urging you to learn from others and then use your own judgement in making decisions.

KNIGDS of SWORDS

**Knight**

Full of life and rampant energy, our young Knight is charging ahead onto the battlefield with no time to formulate a plan or even consider the consequences. His enthusiasm is admirable, but a blind commitment to the task at hand is foolhardy. This card is a warning that only fools rush in where angels fear to tread. Consider all the angles before you act.

**Page**

Another young person, male or female, full of energy and passion and raring to go–but look at all the chaos they leave behind. This card may show up as a sign of impatience and irritation that it's taking too long to get a project off the ground, or when there's something else preventing progress, such a nagging doubt jabbing around the edges of your brain, causing you to question yourself or others.

## Pentacles (also known as Coins or Discs)

This is the suit that is related to the element of earth, so these cards speak to us about manifestations in the physical world, especially material resources and opportunities, including money.

As the cards of the earth, they relate to the astrological earth signs of Capricorn, Taurus, and Virgo. Earth is also considered feminine and receptive.

If you have a reading that is dominated by Pentacles it is likely the questioner has some serious material concerns around their finances, how they make their money, how they spend it, who they share it with, and how to channel their ambitions to realize their material dreams of success and financial security.

**Reading Pentacles: The Royal Court Cards**

KING of PENTACLES

## King

This King has success stamped all over him. He often shows up in a reading to represent someone who is self-made and probably self-employed. Here is someone who likes the finer things in life–we see a castle home in the background–and he has worked hard to earn them. He is materialistic and ambitious, a provider and protector, and anyone associated with him will flourish.

QUEEN of PENTACLES

## Queen

This is a woman of many talents who likes to keep her success private and who does not boast. She has a good business brain along with the good sense to keep her plans to herself. She sits on her throne surrounded by an abundance of bounty and nature, but there is a hidden warning. Notice the rabbit in the right-hand corner, who is there to say, "Be careful where you leap!"

KNIGDS of PENTACLES

**Knight**

Unlike the Knights of the other suits, this one is not chasing off around the world looking for the next blood-thirsty battlefield adventure. He is staying put and doesn't mind being seen as the Steady Eddie of the gang, because he knows, with patience, his efforts will reap the rewards that will make him comfortable in old age. He is responsible and willing to work hard.

PAGE of PENTACLES

**Page**

The single coin (pentacle) we see in the young Page's hand calls for all their focus and attention because it represents ambition, security, wealth, wellbeing, and working with, not against, nature. Look at all the flowers blooming at his feet. He is in no rush because he knows the value of sticking to the task. He tells you that help is available if you ask for it.

## Chapter Summary

- In this chapter we have seen how the Royal Court Cards reflect the core qualities of the suit they belong to. The Wands are linked to Fire (Passion), the Cups relate to Water (Emotions), the Swords represent Air (Intellect), and the Pentacles are assigned to Earth (physical manifestations including money).

In the next chapter we will look at the meanings of the other non-Royal Court Cards, from the Aces to the Tens to see what further clues they can reveal in answer to the question the Tarot reading is asking them.

# Chapter Four: The Other Court Cards

There are ten non-Royal Court Cards in each suit, running from the Ace to the Ten.

We've seen how the different suits represent different aspects of what may be happening in someone's life, so now we are ready to drill down even deeper into how we can read and interpret these remaining 40 cards. Any one of these can show up in even the simplest spread with an important message and guidance for the person asking the question of the Tarot. But before we take a closer look at each card and what it means, let's take a moment to look at the numerology which, as we saw in earlier chapters, can further help us with our interpretations. Numerology traditionally ascribes general meanings to certain numbers and combinations of numbers, and we see these meanings reflected in Tarot.

| Card Number | Theme |
| --- | --- |
| Ace | An important gift is being offered to you |
| Two | Duality & Connection e.g., Mother/Female or Father/Male |
| Three | Growth and Expansion; a period of being busy ahead |
| Four | Consolidation and Stability |
| Five | Control vs Submission and Surrender |
| Six | Security, but also a possible departure |

| | |
|---|---|
| Seven | Reflection/An inner awakening |
| Eight | Boundaries & Limitations |
| Nine | Isolation/Anticipation of something hoped for |
| Ten | A Natural Conclusion (the maximum expression of the suit) |

## Wands

We discovered in our chapter on the Royal Court Cards that Wands are always about passion, communication, and creativity.

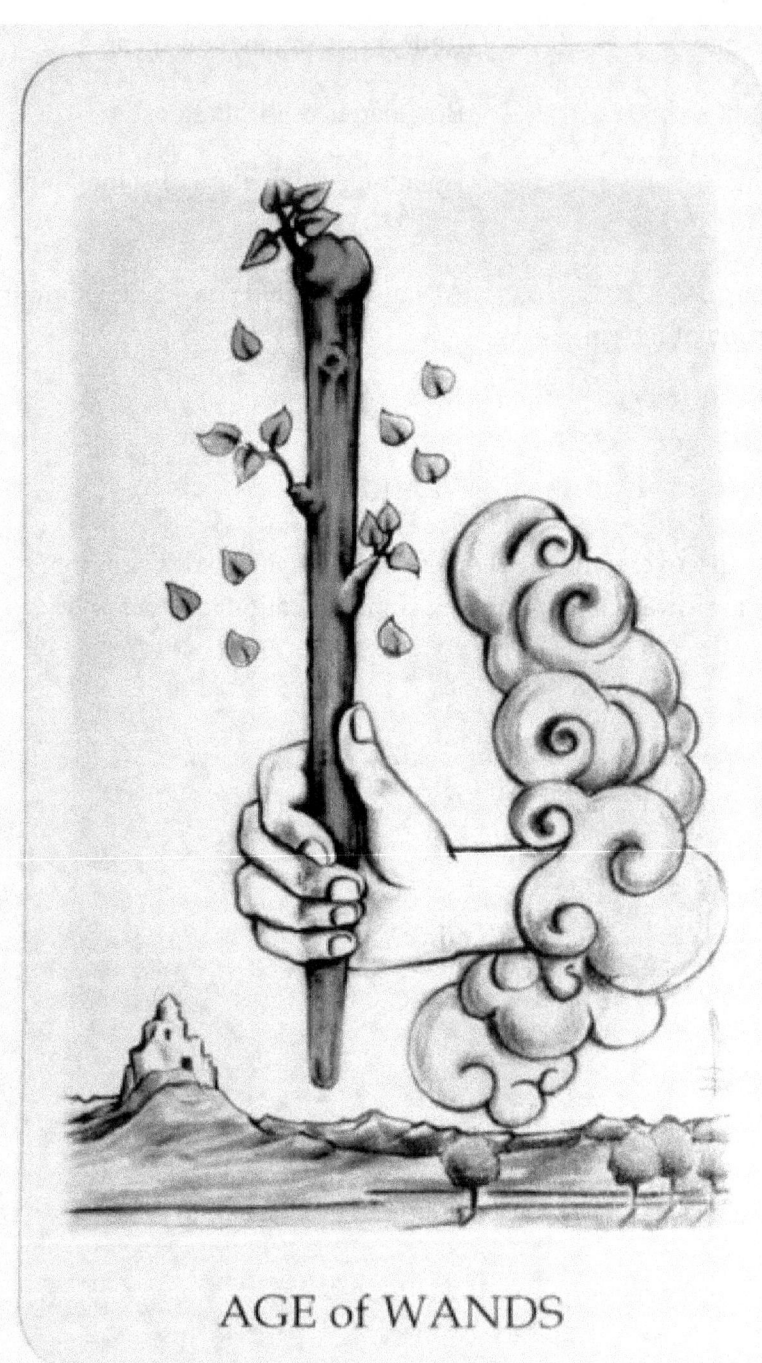

- **Ace:** There is an abundance of creativity available for you once you settle on the right thing to do. You are not on your own—the powers that be are on your side and rooting for you, but this is not a creativity you can learn from others. You must find your own voice and your own way to self-expression. If you pull this card, the message is "Go for it!"

- **Two:** We see a wealthy merchant gazing out over an expanse of water. In his right hand, he holds a globe which speaks of expansion and broader horizons. If you have accepted the gift of being helped to find your voice offered by the Ace, then now may be the time to step out of your comfort zone and expand on your ideas and longer-term goals.

- **Three:** This is a card of foresight and vision. We see another merchant perched high on a hill looking out over all the possibilities ahead. He knows it will take careful planning to execute all that he has in mind for his future and that it is his own hard work that has brought him to this level of success. What lies ahead then is growth and expansion.

- **Four:** A joyful card depicting a shared celebration. We see a happy couple in the foreground and so perhaps it is a marriage that is being celebrated but as ever, with the Tarot, you do not have to be literal. This card can also indicate a celebration that will take place once an important project is completed or just the joy of spending time with family and friends.

- **Five:** Each of the five characters depicted is brandishing their own wand and if you look closely at the faces we can see, nobody looks too happy. That's because there is an argument going on. Is there some kind of conflict in your life, either brewing or already causing sleepless nights? If so, ask yourself what you can learn from it to restore peace and order.

- **Six:** Someone is looking pretty pleased with themselves! We see a young man on horseback riding into town, carrying a wand decorated with a laurel wreath, which tells us this is some kind of triumphant arrival or return. This card is all about success and well-deserved public recognition. Have you received an award at work? If not, there may be one on its way.

- **Seven:** This looks like hard work! Six of the seven wands depicted have been planted in what looks like pretty tough terrain but the seventh has yet to go into the ground. This card is about the struggle you may face to hold on to what you have already achieved. This is not the same as the struggle to get it– it may be harder. Keep your nerve and hold your ground.

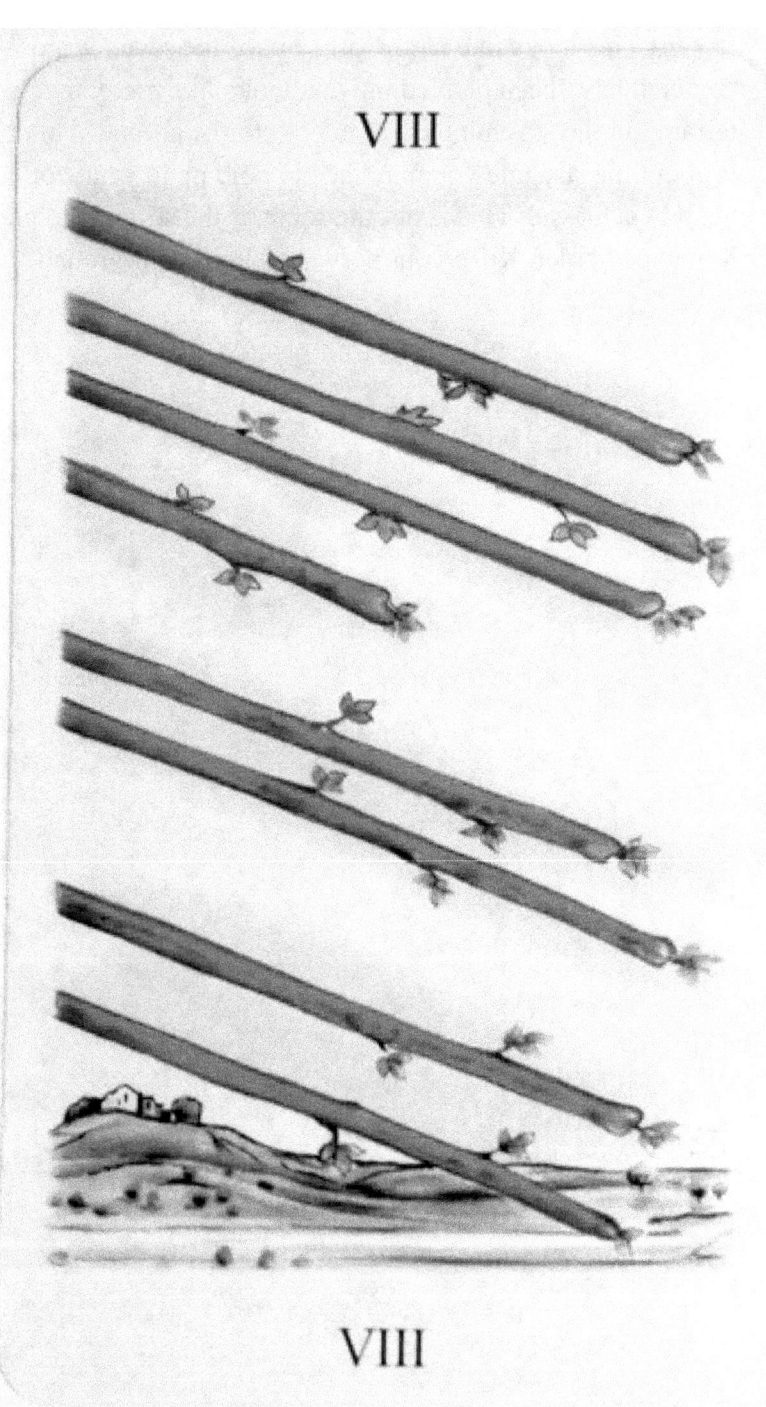

- **Eight:** This is a card that counsels patience, at work or in matters of the heart. Don't force an issue; wait for the right outcome because it is on its way. You have put in the hard work and your ducks (or wands) are lined up and ready to hit their mark. Well done; it has not been easy getting this far. Trust that your hard work is about to pay off.

- **Nine:** Bandaged and still bloody from all those battles you have overcome, you still have hope, so don't give up on whatever it is your heart desires. You may be carrying the deep scars of previous challenges, but what you desire is close and this time, you will know how to keep it once it presents itself. Keep going. Don't fail at the last hurdle.

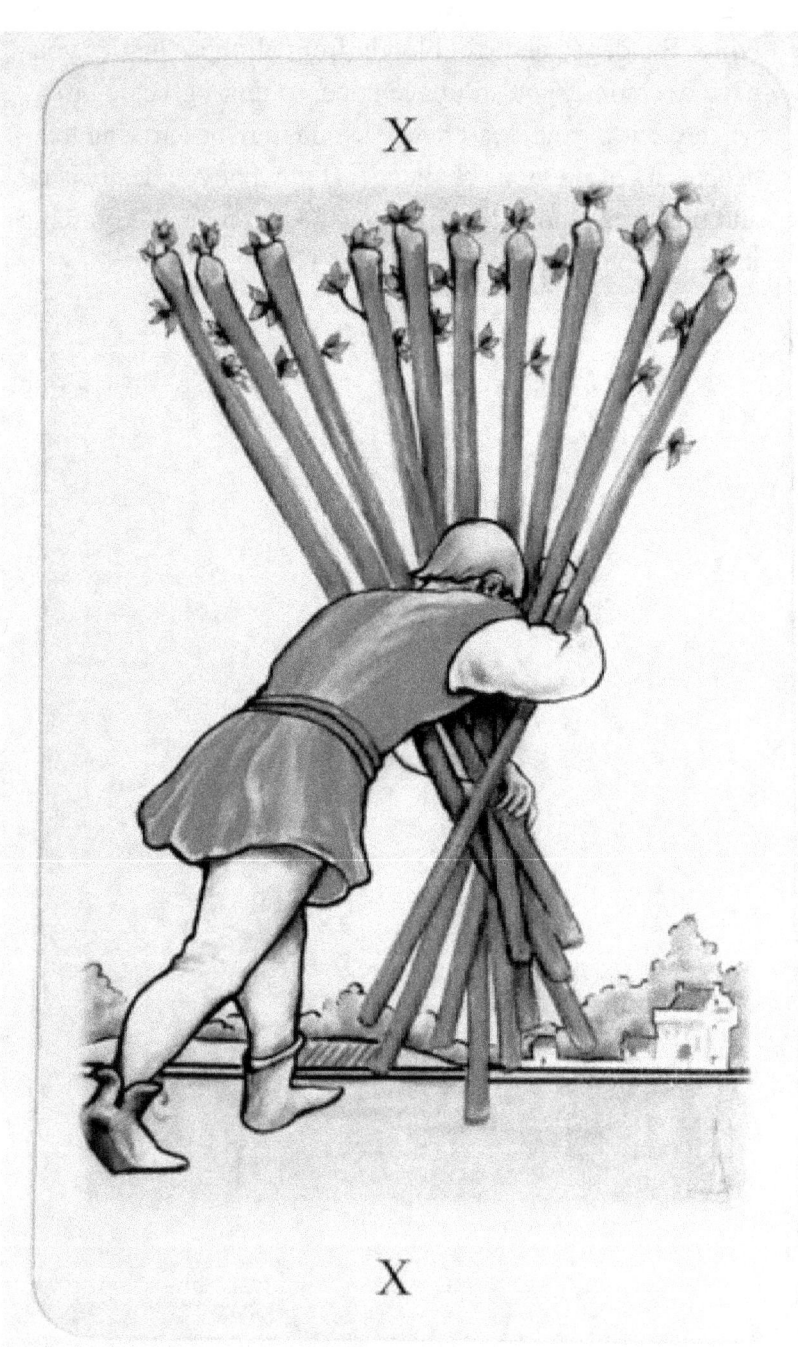

- **Ten:** There is abundance here; we see a man holding on to his horde of 10 wands. But there's also a sense of burden; you've overcome struggles and attained success, but with your success has come great responsibility. You may now have sleepless nights no longer worrying about how to pay the bills, but how to help others. Learn to prioritize.

## Cups

We discovered in our chapter on the Royal Court Cards that Cups are always about our emotions and feelings.

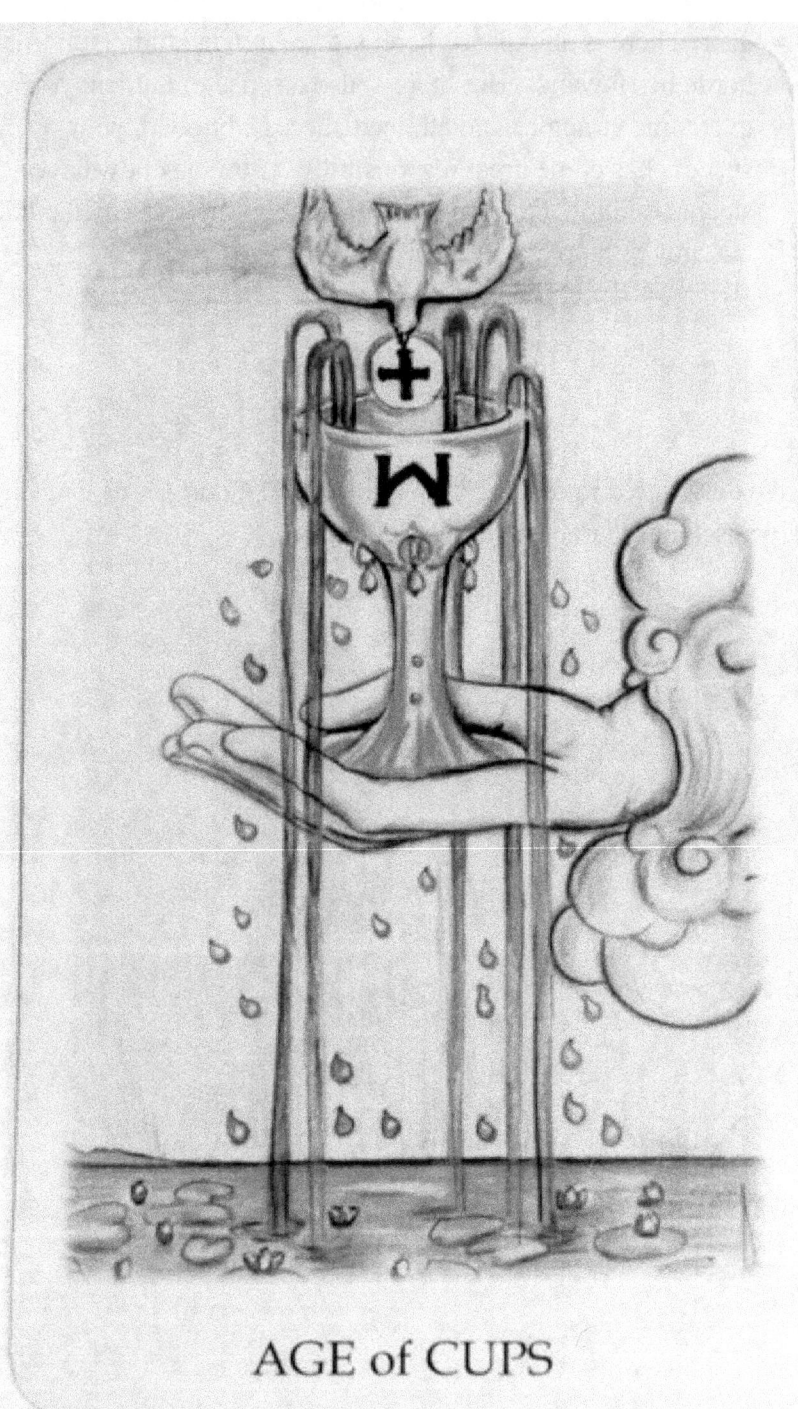
AGE of CUPS

- **Ace:** You're being offered the chance to embrace a new start and take a path that will lead you to great spiritual and emotional fulfillment. The Ace of Cups is brimming over with love and abundance. It's all yours for the asking. Say yes and then listen to your own inner voice, and you will know what steps you need to take next.

- **Two:** We see a couple toasting their success. The winged lion looks on in approval, hovering over the caduceus, which usually signals some kind of partnership, in love or in trade. This will be a strong union between the two parties, and one based on core values of respect, trust, and honorable dealings. Both parties benefit in an equal and respectful way.

- **Three:** The three women celebrating in this scene are happy about something. It could be a wedding or some other family gathering. Whatever the reason, this is a time of happiness. If you have been feeling bereft of good company, this period of drought is about to end. If you have been missing quality time with cherished friends, reunions are coming.

- **Four:** In this scene, there are four cups standing upright in front of the figure of a disconsolate young man who is sitting, arms crossed defensively, at the foot of a tree. He is so lost in thought (and feeling sorry for himself) he cannot see the fourth cup is being offered to help him out of this rut. Start counting your blessings and life will feel less stagnant.

- **Five:** We know from numerology the five cards signify a struggle between surrender and control, and since this card is in the cups suit, this must be an emotional struggle. The three cups toppled over represent serious loss and grief, but our cloaked figure is so focused on these he cannot see that two cups remain upright behind him, revealing that he can move on.

- **Six:** The white flowers growing in each of the six cups symbolize the innocence of childhood. However, not all childhoods were innocent, so while some may have nostalgia for simpler times, for others a childhood was traumatic and painful. The boy offers the girl a flower and the hope of healing if she can let go of those childhood pains.

- **Seven:** This strange scene seems to offer multiple enticements and rewards but look again– each chalice sits on a wispy cloud of fancy and wishful thinking. The true message of this card is to trust your gut and don't be swayed by fantasy, illusion, false promises, or wishful thinking. You know there are more important things in life than material rewards.

- **Eight:** If you have been looking for more meaning in your life and searching for your soul's true purpose, this card tells us you are embarking on the journey. Sometimes it's a perilous journey, but undertaking it shows that you are willing to walk away from the old to achieve that goal. Happily, you have a sturdy staff to keep you on your feet as you move toward higher ground.

- **Nine:** Things are looking up in all the ways that matter; success, a sense of purpose, stability, your health, your money, your relationships, and your happiness. You've overcome grief and loss and other struggles to get to this place of contentment, but don't be tempted to hoard your good fortune. There is no limit on abundance, and you will have your share.

- **Ten:** Ring out the bells, and hang up the bunting! This card shows us the happiness of having it all–family, health, a lovely home and, just as importantly, sharing it with the ones you love. If you are still single, you are about to meet someone who will become important to you. Bring on the good times!

## Swords

We discovered in our chapter on the Royal Court Cards that Swords are always about thinking, decision-making, and the intellect.

AGE of SWORDS

- **Ace:** All the Aces in the Court Cards act as green lights, and this one is no different. What have you been thinking about, planning, or trying to decide? Sometimes the Ace of Swords indicates there is a huge decision to be made and one that will demand innovative action from you. Think outside the box for a chance to conquer new worlds!

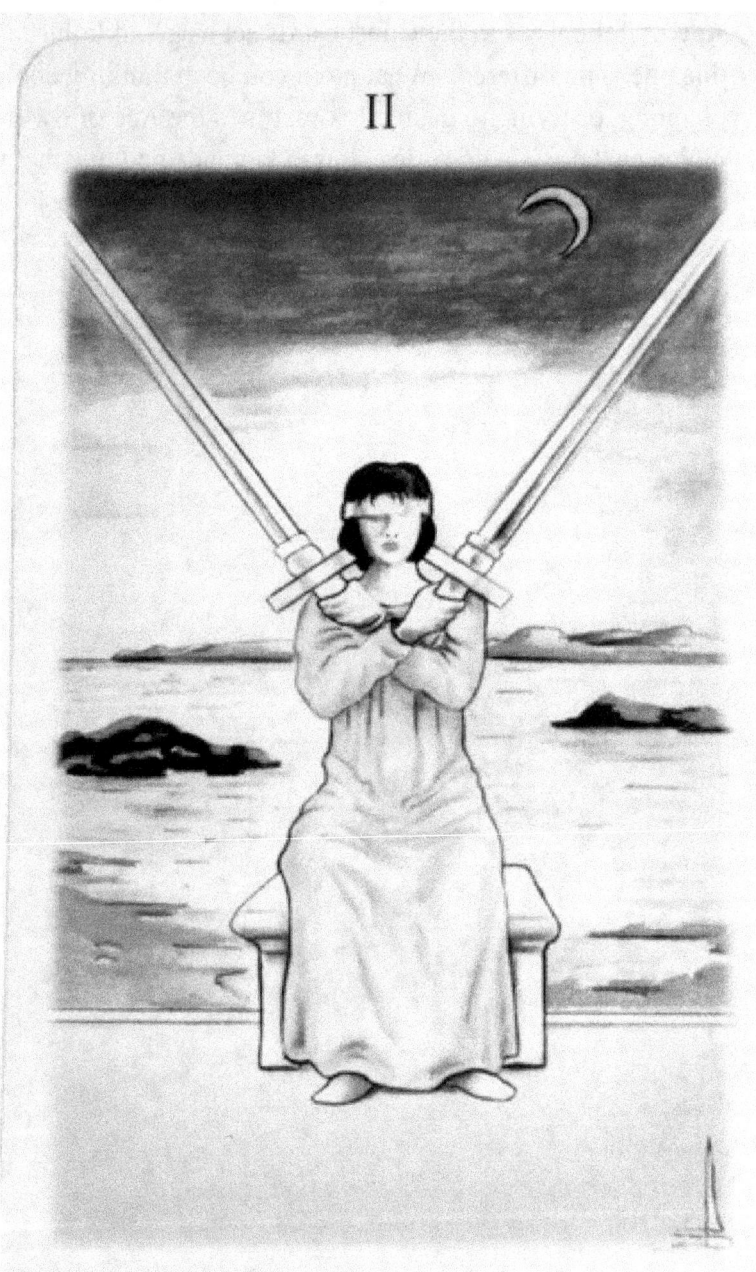

- **Two:** There is a difficult decision to be made, and the fact the woman depicted on this card is blindfolded tells us there is, currently, no clarity about which direction to choose. All we know is that the two paths are mutually exclusive. Don't rush this decision. You will find if you play the waiting game the answer will come naturally.

- **Three:** Without pain and grief, how would we understand the value we should place on joy and happiness? The three of swords is a difficult card depicting horrendous heartbreak following a loss or betrayal or abandonment. Pain is a part of life, but this may be the time to fall back on your intellect and remind yourself that this too shall pass, albeit painfully.

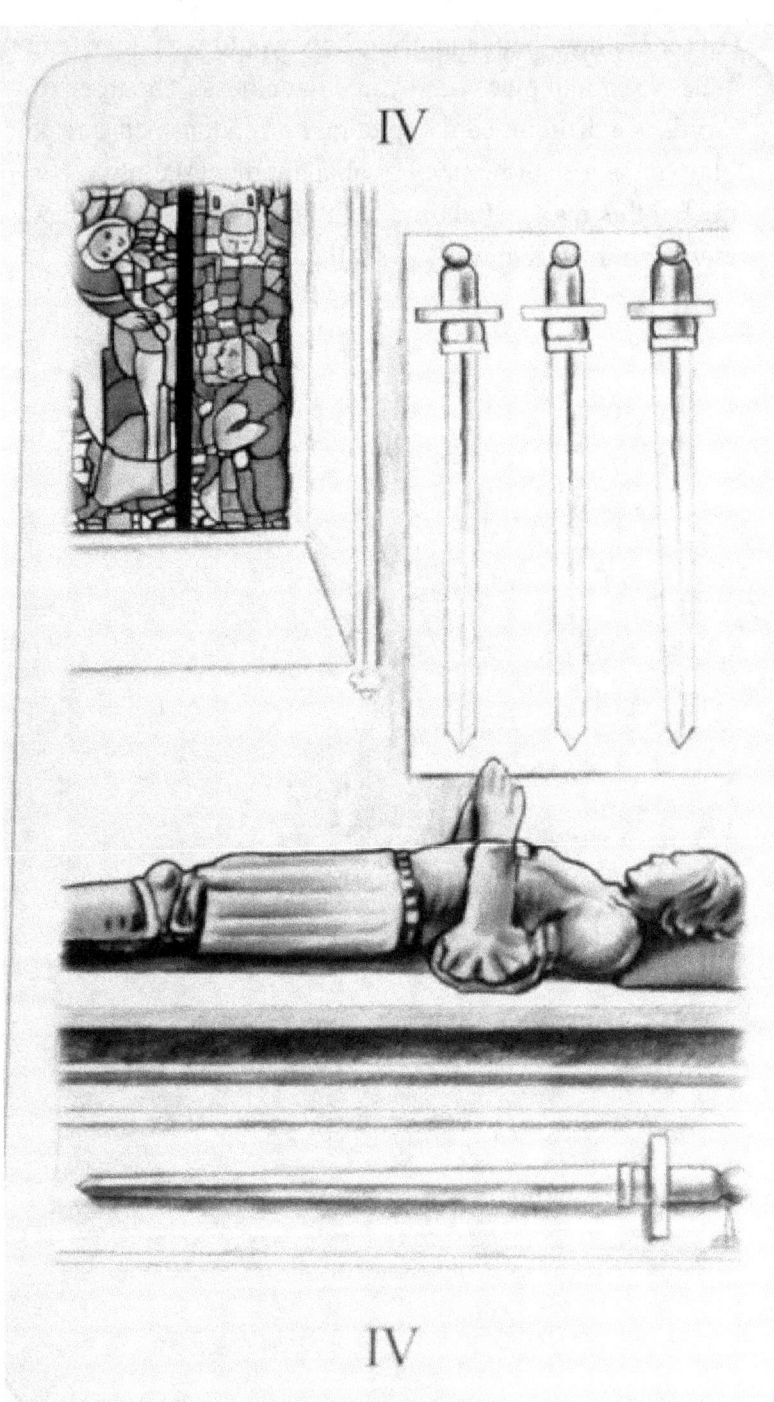

- **Four:** The message of this card is to (metaphorically) put down your sword and retreat in order to rest, recover, and gather the strength to face and fight another day. This card often shows in the reading of someone suffering from psychological challenges including depression. It can be hard to go on when we feel so bleak, but go on we must and will.

- **Five:** After some kind of skirmish, the figure in the foreground now has all five swords at his disposal, and you, likewise, are still standing and have what you need. But was the fight really worth it? The two figures walking away have been hurt and defeated. If you too are now emerging from conflict, take time to take stock, learn the lessons, and avoid it happening again.

- **Six:** The six cards often reveal a departure looming; are you leaving someone or something? There is a big transition afoot, but it's unclear whether the departure is due to change caused by a sorrowful loss or some other event. What does bode well is that the boatman is steering the vessel to a sunnier horizon, so all hope has not been lost.

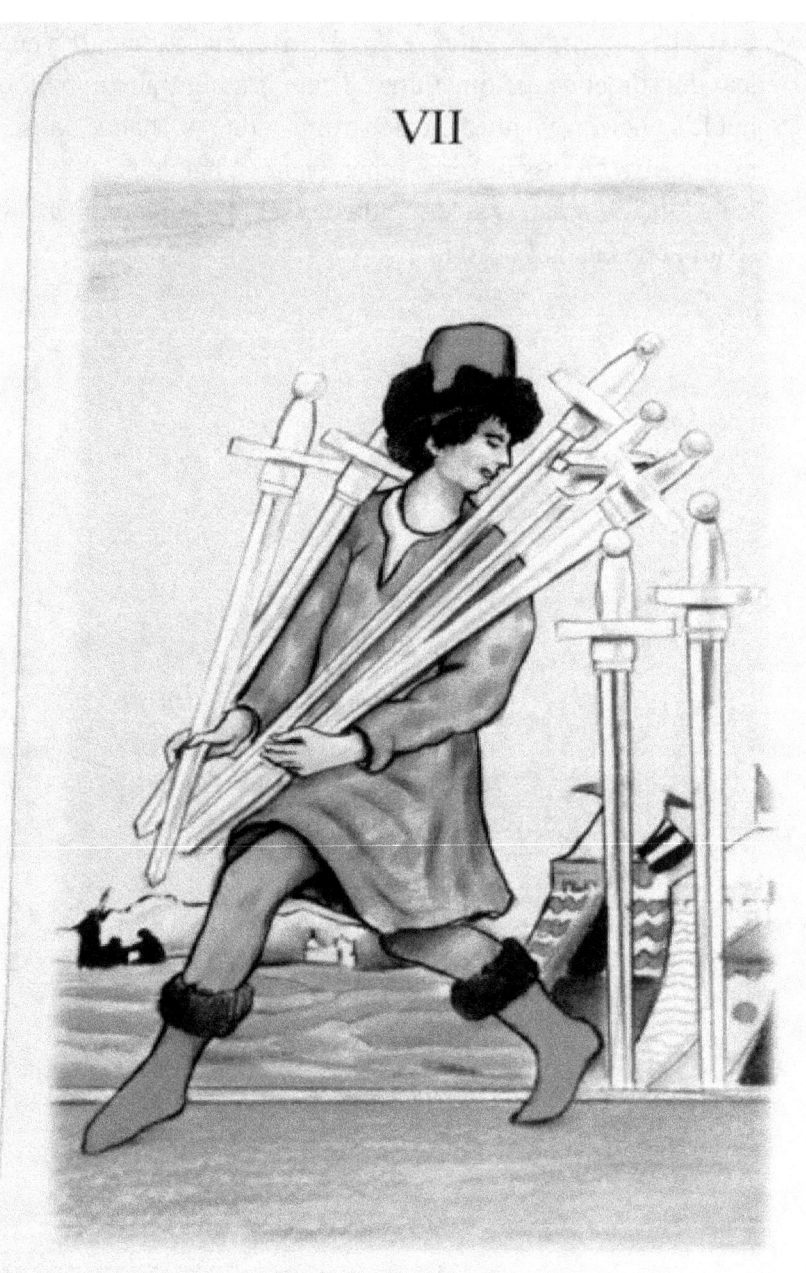

- **Seven:** Are you, or someone you care about, thinking about sneaking away from a difficult situation, rather than bringing it out into the open to confront and resolve? Are you wanting to leave someone or something but lack the courage of your convictions? There's a saying: "You can run but you cannot hide." This is one of those situations.

- **Eight:** This card shows us a blindfolded woman trussed up so she cannot move in any direction. She feels powerless to make any kind of change and that her life is no longer in her own hands. Some people might call this victim thinking, but she believes she has no agency. As soon as she starts to believe otherwise, those bonds will fall away.

- **Nine:** The woman we see sitting up in bed with her head in her hands appears to be at breaking point. Perhaps she is having the same nightmare, over and over, and no longer knows how to break free. Anxiety, fear, depression, and even thoughts of self-harming can be buried, but need to be transmuted and then released so we can move past trauma. Seek help.

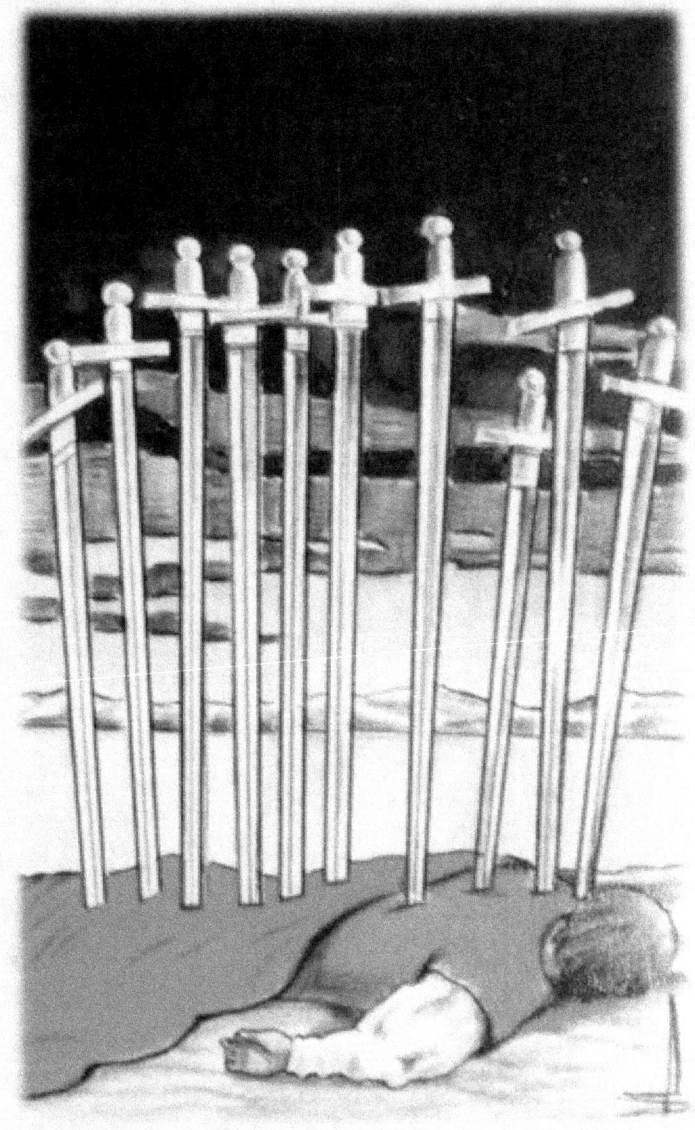

- **Ten:** This is a dark card but take a second look. There is sunlight in the far distance, which is a sign of hope and the dawn of a new day. The figure on the ground has been brutally stabbed in the back. This image can portend some ominous disaster, but more likely it's a metaphor for the way you have punished and harmed your own psyche. Leave that mentality behind.

## Pentacles

We discovered in our chapter on the Royal Court Cards that Pentacles are always about material manifestations, including money and possessions.

AGE of PENTACLES

- **Ace:** A hand offering a large coin hovers over a flourishing landscape, promising abundance, and prosperity. Abundance does not just mean material wealth; it can relate to love, happiness, well-being, and health. A new chapter is beginning for you, a magical one that you will remember forever.

- **Two:** The thing about a juggling act, especially one where the juggler is dancing too, is that it is not sustainable in the long term. Yes, you are managing everything well right now and striking a balance between all the competing demands on your time and money, but this cannot last forever. Move away from the choppy waters we see behind and learn to prioritize before you burn out.

- **Three:** No man is an island, and the three of Pentacles reminds us that the sum of the parts is always greater than the whole. We are invited to join forces with others, especially those who may have a different mindset, to achieve our collective goals and to share wisdom and knowledge for the greater good. Notice how the older characters are seeking advice from the apprentice.

- **Four:** You are now financially stable, but do you have to hang on to your wealth and possessions so tightly that you are not free to do anything else? Where is this fear coming from? You've proven you can weather the storms and work toward your goals, so what's happened to that belief? Dig deep and you will get it back so you can enjoy your successes.

- **Five:** What a sorrowful scene! We see two broken down characters battling through the snow to goodness knows where, both oblivious to the warmth and welcoming glow coming from the window of the church they are passing. Why don't they see help and shelter is right there? Nobody is cursed. There is support available for you, but you have to ask for it.

- **Six:** This is a card that speaks of kindness and generosity, but one which comes with a warning too. We can only give to others, of our time, our money, and our encouragement, when we have taken care of ourselves and have a surplus to give. Otherwise, we can become resentful and mean-spirited. Only give what you can afford to spare; no more and no less.

- **Seven:** This is a card of work and shows us a young man taking stock of his harvest. He will only take what he needs right now; the rest he will invest for his future. You too can be sure of reaping the rewards of your hard work, but only when the time is right. When you do, keep an eye on the future, and put some away for a rainy day.

- **Eight:** Again, a card depicting hard work. This time we have a smithy forging Pentacles in his workshop. He is entirely focused on the task in hand and working away from the distractions of the town in the background. Hard work is commendable but a life with meaning will also make time for rest and relaxation.

- **Nine:** We see a woman who now has the luxury of time to spend in her lush garden, admiring her pet falcon and appreciating the beauty of her surroundings and her great good fortune. She knows who she is, where she has come from, and how she got here. She is independent, living a well-deserved good life.

- **Ten:** We see a snowy-haired grandfather figure, relaxing with his family and dogs, and taking a moment to relish the happy lifestyle he has created through sheer determination. He has not been feckless or expected handouts, and life is good. This card tells you everything will work out.

## Chapter Summary

- We have learned how to look closely at each of the non-Royal Court Cards to begin to understand its symbolism and meaning. As we do this, we can see how a story can start to unfold when we lay out the card in a Tarot spread.

In the next chapter you will learn three easy spreads for beginners.

# Chapter Five: Three Easy Spreads for Beginners

The very simplest Tarot spread is a quick 3-card pull with the first card signifying the past, the second the present, and the third the future. Alternatively, you (or whoever you are reading the cards for) can set a different intent for this reading and decide card one signifies the mind, card two represents the body, and card three speaks of the soul. This is the first, and most simple, Tarot spread you can try.

But before you decide which spread to use, you need first to tap, or shuffle, your cards to ensure they are working to your energy, whether the reading is for you or for someone else.

As with any sacred tool being used for divination work, your Tarot cards are sensitive to the energy of others, so you need to protect them. Keep them wrapped in a soft cloth in a safe place and do not pass them around with the peanuts! Yours should be the only energy infusing the deck, unless you are inviting someone you are reading for to inject their energy and intentions into the space for the reading.

**Tap & Shuffle**

Shuffle your cards as you think about the question you want an answer to. Keep your question short and simple and to the point. Don't throw in complex questions or you will find complex answers which will only serve to confuse. When you are done shuffling, lay the entire pack of cards face down on the table and tap three times with your left hand on the top card to send your energy vibrating down through all the cards.

Use your left hand to tap the cards which symbolically removes the ego from the reading you are about to start.

## Cut The Deck

Once you have tapped your energy into the deck, cut it into three piles. After the first cut, place the pile to the left of the deck and after the second cut, put the cards to the right. Again, use your left hand, to do the cuts.

Now, still using your left hand, reunite the cards in the middle pile onto the left-side pile, pick up this combined pile and place it over the cards on the right side.

You are now ready to choose your cards for the reading.

## Choose Your Spread

As you advance and become more proficient with your cards, you can progress to more complex spreads, but as a beginner, it makes sense to keep things simple. Your real task throughout this book is to get to know your cards.

## Lay Out the Cards Ready for Interpretation

Once you have chosen your spread and the correct number of cards, lay out the spread. When you are ready to do the reading, turn the cards over one at a time, starting with the first card that was chosen and finishing with the last.

# The Celtic Cross

You need 10 cards to lay out the Celtic Cross spread. This spread allows a story to be told about what is going on with regard to a specific question. It can help you understand what may be blocking the outcome you want, what you may need to overcome in order to achieve it, and what the likely outcome will be if you stay on this same path.

Here is how to lay out the Celtic Cross.

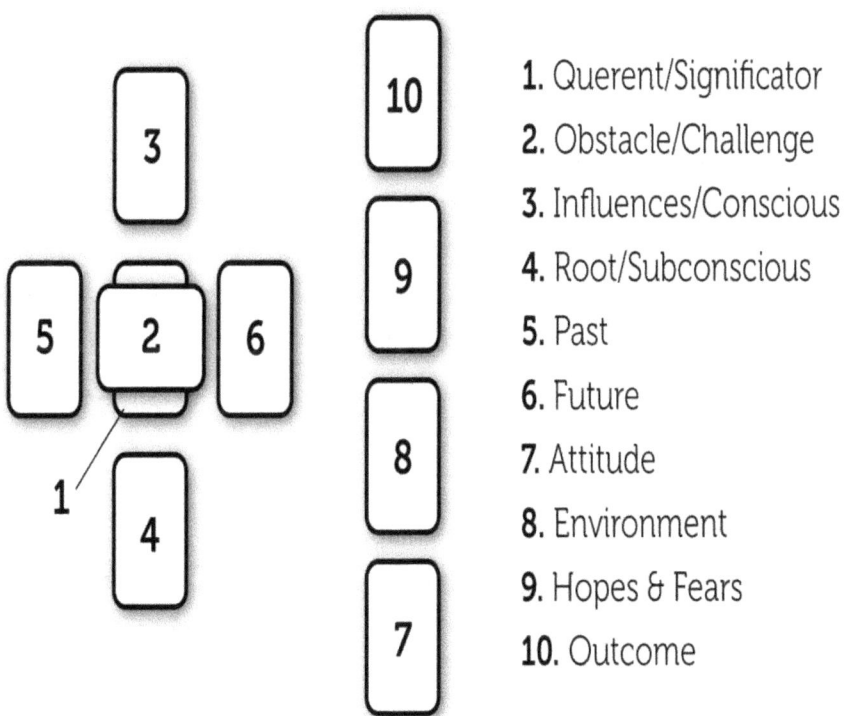

1. Querent/Significator
2. Obstacle/Challenge
3. Influences/Conscious
4. Root/Subconscious
5. Past
6. Future
7. Attitude
8. Environment
9. Hopes & Fears
10. Outcome

The way you read and interpret a Celtic Cross spread is to start with Card 1 and work your way up to Card 10. Take your time to really look at each card, and to consider not only what it means but what the position of the card says about that meaning. Is the card in the present or the past? And even when you know that answer, is it in the far past or the more recent past? The position, once you understand it, will tell you.

Let's work our way through those positions with a real-life example.

*Question: Will I marry again?*

Perhaps the person who this reading is for has been married but is now divorced. We don't know anything else about them, other than they identity as female, and they were previously married to a man.

**Card 1: The Significator**

**Position: In the center of the Celtic Cross**

This card represents the person who is having the reading and the person who has a question they would like the cards to answer. We call this card The Significator.

**Example: The Empress**

This is a mature woman who knows what she wants and who has been used to living the 'Good Life' which may be what she still wants. She is pregnant with possibilities and so marriage may be (literally) on the cards. The Empress frequently signals the start of a new relationship

## Card 2: Obstacles/Challenges

**Position: This card lies horizontally across Card 1**

This card represents problems or obstacles that may be getting in the way of the desired outcome. These can be people, difficult events that have happened, or just fears and anxieties the person having the reading may be struggling with.

**Example: The Knight of Cups**

This card often appears when someone has been so badly hurt that they've learned to keep all their emotions in check and their heart under lock and key. So, what we now know is that the person who this reading is for has learned to play their cards close to their chest and gives very little away.

## Card 3: Influences/Conscious Thinking

**Position: This card lies above Card 1**

This card is all about those things the person asking the questions knows or feels about the issue. In other words, the things they are conscious of. These things are important because they can color or cloud decision-making and judgement. This card gives us the very personal context of this reading.

**Example: Eight of Wands**

This is a card that counsels patience. If the person asking the question is already in a relationship and just wants to know if it will lead to marriage, then the advice this card offers is not to force the issue, but to wait for the right outcome because it is on its way.

## Card 4: Influences/Subconscious Thinking

### Position: Below Card 1

This card shows the root or subconscious factors that may be playing out with regard to the issue. In other words, these are the things the person asking the question does not know consciously. But they do know them subconsciously, so the reading will help bring these factors out into the light to be examined.

### Example: The Hierophant

One of the important Major Arcana, this is the card of convention and tradition, so if the subject of the reading has a relationship, they are subconsciously hoping it will lead to the traditional outcome of marriage. This then tells us their question is more than a casual inquiry; this is what they want.

## Card 5: The Recent Past

### Position: To the left of Card 1

This card says something about what has gone on before which may have led to the current situation.

### Example: The Tower

Again, one of the Major Arcana whose meaning is unambiguous. This person has experienced a dramatic and perhaps sudden end to something that was important in their life. This likely refers to the end of their previous marriage. Even if it was not sudden, the experience was traumatic.

## Card 6: The Near Future

### Position: On the right of Card 1

This card represents the immediate future and what lies just ahead for the person asking the question.

### Example: Queen of Wands

This witchy lady sits strong and upright on her throne. She holds a sunflower, a symbol of success, and a blossoming wand, which symbolizes life. At her feet we see a black cat, which tells us she has hidden depths. The message in this spread is work on yourself, and the rest will naturally come.

## Card 7: Attitude

### Position: Bottom card of the right-hand upright row of four cards

This card reveals what the person asking the question really thinks about the issue; how they feel about it, and how they are responding and reacting.

### Example: Nine of Pentacles

Again, we see a mature woman living the good life and enjoying every second of her achievements and accomplishments. She knows who she is; where she has come from and how she got here. She is independent and, in this spread, her presence suggests a fear of giving up that hard-won independence if a proposal of marriage were to come along.

## Card 8: House & Home

### Position: Directly above Card 7

Sometimes known as the environment card, this card will show us what external factors are having an influence on the issue being explored in the reading.

### Example: Six of Pentacles

The home life is stable and secure, so much so that the person asking the question has a surplus of time/money/energy etc., to give to others. This seems very important to the questioner. They may work as a volunteer or for a charity, and this card tells us they have a strong social conscience. This will be an important factor in any long-term commitment they make romantically.

## Card 9: Hopes & Fears

### Position: This card sits above Card 8

The 9th card in the Celtic Cross spread reveals the hidden hopes and fears of the person having the reading about the issue and the outcome they would like to happen. This card is often one of duality because hopes and fears can exist together over the same thing.

### Example: Temperance

The third Major Arcana card in this spread, Temperance is always about balance. It tells us to find a way to avoid extremes and to walk the middle path. So, with this question, it is saying find a way to maintain your independence and nurture a meaningful relationship. It does not have to be either/or.

## Card 10: The Outcome

### Position: This card sits above Card 9

This card tells us the most likely outcome if everything stays the same and the person asking the question stays on this same path. However, as we discussed previously, the cards do not necessarily predict the future, because once you have more information, you can make different choices, which then change the outcome. The cards can only show you what is likely to happen if you continue as you are now.

### Example: The Page of Pentacles

This is the card that tells the person asking to stop worrying, because they already have everything they need. This card promises security and well-being. If it is marriage the person wants, it will be an option at the right time. The message of this spread is keep doing what you are doing; focus on you and let the rest fall into place around you.

## Summary of a Reading

Once you have examined and interpreted each card in the spread, looking at not only their meaning but their position in the Celtic Cross, you can also check the numerology and scan the cards to see if any one suit is dominant.

With this example reading, seven of the cards have numbers and these add up to a total of 61.

6+1=7

Two of the cards are Pentacles and we have two cards that show mature women living a comfortable life, so we can conclude security and stability is important to the person who has asked if they will remarry.

The overwhelming evidence from the cards, including the Hierophant who speaks of traditions such as marriage, is that they will have this option again and they will say yes. But notice that this is not a prediction. The cards suggest the chances are strong, but at the end of the day, it will be the person who asks the question who decides the outcome.

You can lay out the same cards in the same Celtic Cross as this example so you can better understand how the position of a card influences its interpretation and meaning. For example, if the Knight of Cups had been the 10th and final card, and not Card 2, then the conclusion of this story would have been very different.

The Knight of Cups shows us someone who is scared to give their heart away. The conclusion would have been it would be unlikely you will remarry unless you do the work to unlock your heart so you can share your emotions and believe in love again.

# The Inverted Pyramid Spread

Lay out your 10 cards in an inverted pyramid with the first card you chose at the bottom and the last one you chose at the end of the four cards on the top row.

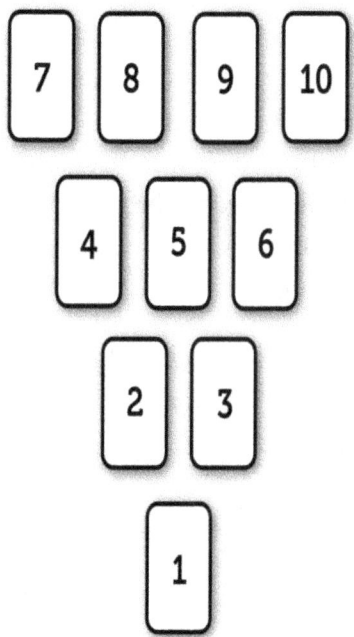

Row 1: Single card = Significator (You or the person you are reading for)

Row 2: Two cards = Dilemma/Dichotomy (the essence of the problem underlying the question)

Row 3: Three cards = Past, Present, Near Future (how things stand now)

Row 4: Four cards = Coming Up, and so this will be the conclusion of this story i.e. What will happen next if this trajectory stays the same.

The Inverted Pyramid spread is useful for following a story through the reading and, as with the Celtic Cross, it starts with the person asking the question, reveals what the real issues underlying the question are, tells us what is going on right now following recent past events, and what will happen next if the querent stays on this same tract. The final card of the top row (the card on the right of the top of the pyramid) tells us the outcome that can be expected based on the cards that have gone before.

With this spread, the first card laid down should be the first card the subject has selected, and the final card (top row, right-hand card) should be the last card chosen.

Start your reading on the bottom row and think about what this card tells you about you or the person you are reading for. What scene is playing out? What are the themes that govern the number of this card?

Get a real sense of who is asking the question and when you're ready, move to the second row, which will reveal more about why this specific question is being asked.

## Chapter Summary

- This chapter has shown you there are multiple choices when it comes to deciding which spread to use to read the cards. Eventually, you will settle on a favorite spread but as a beginner, it is a good idea to try out different options and see which one you resonate with most.

In our final chapter you will find some more expert advice on deepening your connection to the Tarot cards and, as a result, learn to develop the art of Tarot reading with your interpretations.

# Chapter Six: Reading the Cards

**At-a-Glance Interpretations**

There are so many cards in the Tarot deck you cannot expect to learn their meanings overnight. As with any divination practice, the meanings are never set in stone but, as we have learned, will be interpreted based on:

(1)   The question being asked/the intent that has been set
(2)   The card's position in the chosen spread
(3)   The cards that lead up to the card being interpreted, as well as the cards that follow
(4)   The Tarot deck you have chosen to work with
(5)   Your intuition
(6)   Your growing skills as a Tarot reader

The best way to learn the cards is to adopt a daily practice of choosing three cards at random from the deck and taking the time to sit with them.

Really look at each card. Look closely at all of the details depicted in the image you see but also, try to tune in to the card itself. Notice what you feel in relation to that card and the image shown. To help you do this, ask yourself some of the following questions:

- Does this card make you feel sad or happy?
- Are the people depicted celebrating or bleeding from a bloody battle that has just taken place?
- Are there any animals shown and if so, what is their meaning?
- Is there a powerful central character like the Magician or the High Priestess?

- Does it feel as if this card may carry a warning of some kind?
- Do you think the card is showing there may be adventure ahead?

Don't limit yourself to these questions, and feel free to come up with your own. The idea behind this daily practice is to familiarize yourself with each of the 78 cards. The best way to do this is to spend time with them, so that when a card shows up in a spread, you already have a relationship with that card and know how to interpret it at a glance.

It is important to remember there are no absolutes when it comes to understanding and reading the Tarot. This relationship you are building with your cards will be unique and personal to you. It is true that each deck comes with a small booklet suggesting interpretations, but the world has moved on since the design of the classical Rider Waite deck. You will want to put a more contemporary interpretation on images that have their roots in medieval times.

For example, if you are looking at the Page of Wands, and you remember that wands signify communication and that the Page card is usually a sign of anticipation, you will more likely think there is an important email or WhatsApp message on its way, not a snail-mail letter or delivery by pigeon post!

**Reversed Cards**

When you consult the booklet that comes as part of your new Tarot deck you will see that it includes interpretations for when the card appears in the spread upside down, or reversed. You will find the same in other books and guides but in truth, the whole idea of reversed cards is not one that is accepted by all Tarot readers.

There are some contemporary readers who believe reversed cards were used in a somewhat manipulative way to scare people who were paying for their readings into coming back for further readings in order to try and correct their course as was depicted in the cards and avoid misfortune.

It will be entirely your choice as to whether you wish to include a reading of reversed cards in your work at some stage but for now, as a beginner, it makes better sense to learn the upright meanings of the cards before complicating your readings with reversals.

I never deal reversed cards, but always ensure my cards are upright in my deck before I shuffle and lay out my chosen spread for a reading. You can also simply choose to read all cards as upright, whether they present themselves upside down or not.

This is, in large part, because I see the Tarot as a useful tool to open up a conversation about psychological issues that may otherwise stay buried, but still be affecting life choices in a more insidious way. In other words, Tarot can bring these issues into the light for further reflection or discussion, which means your ongoing choices, or those of the person you are reading for, can then be more informed.

**Reading the Numbers**

If you are interested in numerology, then you can bring the significance of numbers into your Tarot reading too. As you familiarize yourself with the cards, pay attention to their individual numbers (only the Fool has no number), and then further interpret the card based on its number. At the end of the reading, you can then interpret the spread based on adding together the numbers of all the cards that have shown up in order to discover the ruling number of the reading.

If you have had little or nothing to do with numerology, don't worry. Once you have added all the numbers of the individual cards together to come up with a total, then add the numbers in that total to get a figure of below 9.

For example, if you do a 10-card pyramid spread and your total number from all the cards is 54 then add 5+4=9 so the number ruling this spread is the number 9, which is always about endings.

**Reading the Major Arcana**

Remember when you are interpreting a spread, the Major Arcana speak of the bigger themes, triumphs, or challenges in the life story–past, present or future–and that what they say trumps everything else. Scan your spread first for these cards and make a note of their positions and what they indicate as a likely outcome if you stay on this same trajectory.

Take your time to engage with the story being told and the themes/archetypes being explored in this reading. There is no clock ticking; you are learning, and learning takes time and practice.

**Reading the Minor Arcana**

Once you have identified and considered the significance of the Major Arcana, take a look at the Minor Cards you have chosen and see if you can see how these may relate to the bigger themes. The Minor Arcana speak to us of the more everyday influences shaping our lives and the paths we take, so look for clues about love, money, relationships, and opportunities that may be coming.

Remember to consider the individual numbers of the cards and at the end of the reading, add all the numbers together to help you understand the overriding theme of this story. Are the cards coming together to tell you there is a new start ahead or are they asking you to think about issues of control versus surrender?

Go back to the table of numbers in chapter four to remind yourself what the numbers mean.

## Telling the Whole Story

The art of Tarot reading can only develop with practice, patience, and time. Getting to know the cards and their meanings is the first step; the second is building your own relationship with the cards in whichever deck you choose to work with. Remember to nurture and cherish that relationship so that it deepens over time.

One thing you will need to practice is working out the story that is playing out in a spread. Keep this simple at first. Start at the beginning with the first card that was selected and work out what this card relates to. Is it a person, a situation, or someone from your past?

Once you have the answer to this question, you can use this card as your psychic jumping off point and start to follow the story.

Experiment with the different spreads in this chapter and when you are ready, branch out and try new and different spreads until you find the one(s) you like best and are happiest working with.

If you are following a story that suddenly veers off with the appearance of an unexpected card or one that does not make sense, don't panic. Reading the cards together is an art and you can always come back to this card once you have spent more time looking at and thinking about the other cards in the spread.

Every card is there for a reason. Every card has something to say to you.

Remember that when we learn anything new, we move forward in fits and starts, and sometimes, we move backwards before we take a giant leap into a new level of understanding.

Trust this process. Much of what the cards have to say will be said to your subconscious, and your job then is to relax enough to trust that the more you allow it, the more these meanings will become clear.

Eventually, you will look at a card or a spread and you will just know.

And when that happens, you are no longer a beginner!

## Chapter Summary

- In this final chapter, you have started to deepen your relationship with the Tarot. The more you do this, the more you will understand that the best readings and interpretations happen when we leave ego and expectation outside the door and allow ourselves to tune in to the cards so we can hear what they have to say to us. There are no rights and wrongs; trust yourself and listen as closely as you can to what these wonderful cards have to say just to you.

# Conclusion

Congratulations on making it to the end of this book! By now, you should have a good understanding of Tarot, its origins, and what each of the different cards represent.

As with any new skill, learning to become proficient at reading the Tarot will take some practice. This can be by doing readings on yourself, or by practicing on friends and family.

With time, you will become faster and more accurate with your readings, particularly as your connection with your Tarot deck grows.

I hope you have enjoyed learning about the art of reading the Tarot, and are excited to begin practicing this amazing skill on your own!

www.ingramcontent.com/pod-product-compliance
Lightning Source LLC
LaVergne TN
LVHW021714060526
838200LV00050B/2660